By the same author

Tongue without Hands (*Dolmen Press*)
Expansions (*Dolmen Press*)
Faoistin Bhacach (*An Clóchomhar*)
Josep Carner: 30 Poems (*Dolphin Books, Oxford*)—from Catalan
Friend Songs: Medieval Love-Poems (*New Writers Press*)—from Galaicoportuguese

Pearse Hutchinson

Watching The Morning Grow

Gallery Books
Dublin

Watching the Morning Grow is published in a limited edition of 2,000 copies, 300 of which are bound in cloth and signed by the author, by

The Gallery Press,
(Editor: Peter Fallon),
19 Oakdown Road,
Dublin 14. Tel. 985161.

© Pearse Hutchinson 1972

This book is published with the assistance of
An Chomhairle Ealaíon (The Arts Council of Ireland).

Acknowledgements

To the editors of *An Deoraí Gaelach* (Leeds), *Aquarius* (London), *Capella*, *The Dublin Magazine*, Hayden Murphy's *Broadsheet*, *The Lace Curtain*, *Litter* (Dartington), *Misery Hill* (San Francisco), *New Irish Writing* (The Irish Press), *The Pleiades Burst into Tears*, *Ploughshares* (Cambridge, Mass.), *Poetry and Audience* (Leeds), *The Poetry Workshop Broadsheet* (UCD), *Soundings '72*, *Two Rivers* (London), and *The Unfree Citizen*, in which some of these poems have appeared.

Contents

Ringing the changes on Mistral	*page* 9
Gaeltacht	10
Quinze juillet, early morning	12
Seán O'Sullivan	13
Secret	14
Lyde	15
Sadlers Farm	16
Cotswold Nightflower	17
Poem with Justin for Paul and Nessa	18
Into their true gentleness	20
Geneva	21
Mama Poule	22
Not Clegs but Nightmares	23
Ireland 1970 Bolivia Year of Our Lords the Colonels Glasses Glinting	24
Pub Song	26
Death-Washing	27
Belfry-Hunting	28
The Jailing of Devlin	30
Ageing	31
I stole a march and you stole a coaster; black to a bright room	32
A True Story	34
Like Trees, like Islands	35
Connemara	36
Sometimes Feel	37
Homage to José Martí	38
A Rose and a Book for Sant Jordi	39
Ode to the Future	40
The black and white of this world	42
Bright after Dark	43
Lovers	44
It still happens	45
Notes	46

To Maurice O'Dwyer
1932-1972

Ringing the changes on Mistral

My mother brought me forth to show,
the neighbors came and gave me

a couple of eggs,
a cut of bread,
a grain of salt,
and a match-stick,

telling me to be:

as full as an egg,
as good as bread,
wise like salt,
straight as a match.

And if I later became
as empty as a cracked eggshell,
as bad as bread gone green,
foolish as caked salt,
and pointless like a spent match,

recall, as in Paris partridge
is less than apples at home,
that once I may have been

egg-full,
bread-good,
salt-wise,
match-straight.

Gaeltacht

Bartley Costello, eighty years old,
sat in his silver-grey tweeds on a kitchen chair,
at his door in Carraroe, the sea only yards away,
smoking a pipe, with a pint of porter beside his boot:
"For the past twenty years I've eaten nothing only
periwinkles, my own hands got them off those rocks.
You're a quarter my age, if you'd stick to winkles
you'd live as long as me, and keep as spry".

In the Liverpool Bar, at the North Wall,
on his way to join his children over there,
an old man looked at me, then down at his pint
of rich Dublin stout. He pointed at the black glass:
"Is lú í an Ghaeilge ná an t-uisce sa ngloine sin".

Beartla Confhaola, prime of his manhood,
driving between the redweed and the rock-fields,
driving through the sunny treeless quartz glory of Carna,
answered the foreigners' glib pity, pointing at the
small black cows: "You won't get finer anywhere
than those black porry cattle". In a pub near there,
one of the locals finally spoke to the townie:
"Labhraim le stráinséirí. Creidim gur chóir bheith
ag labhairt le stráinséirí". Proud as a man who'd claim:
"I made an orchard of a rock-field,
bougainvillea clamber my turf-ricks".

A Dublin tourist on a red-quarter strand
hunting firewood found the ruins of a boat,
started breaking the struts out—an old man came,
he shook his head, and said:
"Áá, a mhac: ná bí ag briseadh báid".

The low walls of rock-fields in the west
are a beautiful clean whitegrey.   There are chinks between
the neat stones to let the wind through safe,
you can see the blue sun through them.
But coming eastward in the same county,
the walls grow higher, darkgrey:
an ugly grey.   And the chinks disappear:
through those walls you can see nothing.

Then at last you come to the city,
beautiful with salmon basking becalmed black below
a bridge over the pale-green Corrib; and ugly
with many shopkeepers looking down on men like
Bartley Costello and Beartla Confhaola because they
speak in Irish, eat periwinkles, keep
small black porry cattle, and on us
because we are strangers.

Quinze juillet, early morning

A woman walking swiftly
along a moving barge,
an earthen-colored crane
eternally revolving,
the big sand-colored stones
dropping like jewels on the off-white stone,
the woman walking swiftly to the prow.

The private victory at quiet tables
over the slightly disappointing festival,
a half-misguided longing
for warm food and lovers,
the quai petering out in a cluttered desert
of trees and railings, iron rails and trains.

The sun between the trees, the momentary cold,
the colored night as if it had not been;
a poem, like a breast, firming swiftly
under a quiet, an excited hand.

Seán O'Sullivan

for Carl Ordonez

He passed out in the pub.
People he may have thought
were friends began to talk about him;
not kindly. (Perhaps they
were friends.)
After a time he woke up,
stood up
to his great height, glared
down at them,
down;
and said, not raucous but emphatic
(echoing round the weekday afternoon):
"Ceapann sibh go bhfuilim as mo mheabhair".
Then he sat down again,
and passed out again.

Few men ever had
more beautiful Gaelic, a richer voice.

And in a different pub, one day he was more or less sober,
and I was drunk, and under trouble
from the savages
(not the ones in me
but the others, their quislings),
he spoke to me kindly.
Amid savagery so deep
I dare not name it.
That single brief kind sentence held
more courage, more sadness, and grace
than most men manage in a lifetime.

So for him, who was not called my friend
but called an acquaintance,
I keep the kind thought waving
its three inverted commas
round about wildly
somewhere inside my barbarity.

Secret

They made an idol of this man, because
he did not have to break any to prove
there were none. But that was what he did
prove: that there were no idols.
So they made an idol of him.

They shouted subtle maudlinities about
his lack of sentimentality.
They wept happy cataracts of words,
frozen as melting snow, hard as turkish
delight, about his granite eye.

In this way, it remains a dowdy secret
that only his earth-sized, meticulous capacity
for admiration keeps him free of idols;
and the granite glory of his unrelenting eye
could not have been reared and lit by anything but love.

Lyde

tibi,
with corni da caccia

In the summer morning when I awake at six
   from crisp green sheets and blue, clear-headed after cider,
a squirrel is playing on the grass gently sloping
   down from house to brook. Dark, tough-looking birds jabbing
at bread left out in a long tin on a low table;
   rusty baking-dish on broken brown marble, a feeding.
The flowers near the brook's edge not doing so well:
   deer come out of the trees at dawn to eat the heads,
leaving only their footprints. I trot, clear-headed,
   across the dew to inspect the prints but cannot,
rude suburban, find them (school never toyed with nature).
   Creaking back through glass doors, easily find the pottle,
relieved a little still left, relieved it's only a little,
   not enough to be sozzled by mid-morning: enough
to drink slow, but not mingily, two long glasses
   watching the morning grow: squirrels, birds, a rumor
of antlers back there, somewhere, in the dense woods for
   a thrill—easy? cheap? Things ought to be easy and cheap
once in a while, even often, like this peace here
   given to me by friends, watching the sun make over
the long narrow water, the trees—I name those I know:
   beech, alder, ash, elm (All vowels alliterate),
I must ask my friend the name of the other trees,
   I'll ask him when the child awakes and is fed, when
the grown-up breakfasts are taken, the flower-heads tied
   in fishing-net against the deer—for soon we leave,
three for Italy, one for Bristol: exciting
   places! and so they are. But for me peace here now
is more than excitement, so between six and eight
   on a July morning I nurse the yellowish drink,
the green and blue nylon sheets, the Gloucester sunlight,
   the creatures. Feel gratitude (my own: not imposed),
mean love (perhaps could make it mine), one brief dry retch
   of envy (that's mine for sure), then relax. Relax
at last. No shame, here, yet, for taking some peace.
   What else do the starving and the tortured want?
Bread in a baking-tin, sun upon brown, a feeding

Sadlers Farm

Shaped like the bearskin on a guardsman's head,
with, in the top right corner, a slight dent,
the vast sycamore makes a one-tree forest
in the hollow between two grassy hillocks.
A field away, it fills my attic window,
and on this almost windless day no stir
of leaves can I detect, unless perhaps
near the centre where a little blue comes clear.
No trunk is seen, no twigs, no wood: all is green
except that saving patch of distant blue.
From the hollow the tree rises compact
like a crannóg from a Leinster lake.

Seen from elsewhere, some distance to the left
and lower down: from a green seat—Italian
plastic, the kind you blow up—the sycamore's
unique massive impact is part-concealed
by a leafless derelict-looking apple-tree
and eight black-and-white cows, chewing standing up.

Resentful of these obscuring things, I leave
down beer and book, and cross the grass, and climb
the white ladder to the white attic, to place
the sycamore back inside its right frame,
that small but perfect window. A maroon moth,
light-lured last night, seemed, on entering,
to fill my attic window, so that now
sycamore and moth make a full day.

Cotswold Nightflower

A bright flower in a cold night
implies a glow, the dandelion
recalls a yellow fire,
illusive warmth breaks through
the huddling sheets, keeps out
the howling wind scouring house
and ground—the yellow beak
of a blackbird pecking blizzard grass.

Poem with Justin for Paul and Nessa

Paul you brought us in
Nessa said Come to us

At three in the morning she said
Come to us
At four in the morning
you opened your door to us

At three in the morning
by four broken phones
by one phone that worked
by two lucky sixpenny bits
by five cruising taxis who turned us away
by one taxi that took us
by two bloodsoaked hankies
dropt on the nightmare street
by a long desolate street
by fear of pursuers to finish the job
we didn't know which way to turn
we didn't know which way led to you
at four in the morning
by grace of friendship
by grace of poetry
by grace of marriage
we came to you

We came home to you Paul
Nessa we came homing
Sara / Síafra
did we wake you up?
We came home

By grace of electricity
by grace of petrol
by grace of greed
by grace of money
we crossed London

When we got to your gate
your window was lit
you were standing there already
in the lighted doorway

at the open door
at the OPEN door

You brought us in you looked after us
you gave us a drink and a place to sleep
you listened

You washed my face gently
you washed the blood from swelling flesh

At three in the morning
in the terrifying city
well within hearing of the beast
by four broken phones
by two lucky sixpenny bits
by two red hankies
by the rending pain of coughing through beaten ribs
by the broken sleeping of two small children
by the strength of two tired people
not too tired
we came to you

Out of despair
onto a skellig of hope

Oh it was difficult landing
but you made it easy
out of your difficulty
we had it easy

Whatever blood whatever grime
I snuffle stumble blubber through
from now till the bloodstained hanky
drops in my nightmare street
I'll get washed in memory clean
made whole again
by Nessa telling us Come
by Paul standing waiting
at the lighted open door.

                        october/november 70
                        london-dublin

Into their true gentleness

for Katherine Kavanagh

If love is the greatest reality,
and I believe it is,
the gentle are more real
than the violent or than
those like me who
hate violence,
long for gentleness,
but never in our own act
achieve true gentleness.
We fall in love with people
we consider gentle,
we love them violently
for their gentleness,
so violently we drive
them to violence,
for our gentleness
is less real
than their breaking patience,
so falsely we accuse
them of being false.

But with any luck,
time half-opens our eyes
to at least a hundredth
part of our absurdity,
and lets them travel back,
released from us,
into their true gentleness,
even with us.

Geneva

for Bob Welch

The silver curving fish
upon the shining florin

Bent nearly double as they leant
over the parapet small boys
with home-made tackle caught
in as many minutes five
little silver shining fish
out of the green Rhone.

The silver curving salmon
upon the shining florin

The naked stone horsemen
proud on their tall pediments
flanked the long broad bridge
I watched the intent
excited anglers

An old man with a brown bald head
cried encouragement
and one of the boys who wore
a blue-and-white cap
crimson-tasselled
and clean white socks
crowed non-stop
in a shrill voice:
O ma petite
as the little fish came
swirling up on the line
lost for ever
to the clean green water
O ma petite, ma petite

Mama Poule

Mama Poule, as few called him, was invited to a party. Before the invitation was confirmed he had to pass through many tests, of a rigor comparable to those undergone in ancient Ireland by candidates for the Fianna, to prove himself for real. In the end he scraped through, and the party was unbelievably beautiful. So after that he went to many such, in various parts of this gob of laughter. But one night, on his way to one of these shindigs, he met in the street a girl he'd been at co-ed school with, a nice harmless girl who thought she liked camp. They hadn't seen each other for a decade, she told him she'd just come back from Athos, and suddenly a great nostalgic tenderness billowed up inside him and he asked her along to the party—knowing full well that, unlike Athos, no women were allowed; but hoping for once that ghettoes might be kinder than laws and customs.

Needless to say, they were both booted down the front steps at sight, by a hearty disguised as a non-hearty. Mama Poule saw the girl to a taxi (as usual, the last bus had just gone) and walked around in the somnolescent city, to see could he sober up and quieten down. He could not. So feeling closer to despair than ever before, even in the proudest quagmires of romantic love, he went to a sheebeen where he drank a great deal of bad whiskey out of coffee-cups.

He woke on a bench in Parnell Square, his arm round a sleeping whore. As dawn was breaking he saw that she had no nose. He left her there, and boarded the next plane for Granada, where he spent a long time trying in vain to kill pigeons in the public squares.

Not Clegs but Nightmares

When Franco's imperial crusaders,
puffing up their merkined nobilities,
having pacified Pamplona
a cristazos limpios,
reconquered Catalunya, Durruti
was already dead and buried.   Thwarted
they refused to be thwarted but dug
"Durruti" up, tied his corpse to
a tree and a firing-squad
shot the corpse dead.

When Vassili Nikiforovich Chadayev
was killed by hired guns beside a road in
the Kuban his friends would have waked him
in Leningrad, the city he loved,
for he'd fought in the Rising of '17.
But this was not allowed:
he'd been exorcized from the Party:
a stone, with an inscription,
built on the spot where he died,
was broken into smithereens.

When some human beings fled Belfast
through menace in the holocaust
August of '71
they were stoned in the station as they waited
for a train down to comparative peace,
to a lesser inferno.   These
are not yet utterly killed.   But what more
did those dead stones need?
Or dream to breed?   In vain?

Ireland 1970 Bolivia Year of Our Lords the Colonels Glasses Glinting

for Pere Quart

We've seen
a golden spine,
the twin birth of pine-needles,
riverbanks yellow with oranges,
the brightblue, tumbling Clady,
dawn down a valley.
We've been
to Amadora, Pnom-Penh,
Baggot Street Bridge, Athy.
We've known
a man worth more than his work.
We've dreamt
a man who never said mine.

We listened
to Constantino Suasnavar
translating Carleton
from Gaelic into silence.
Tenderness became manhood,
even daily.
We listened
to a small stone face in a chapel
serene but gabbling
across time.

Green lizard.   Red seaweed.
A man in prison
freed us with his music.
We sprang to Farandouri.
We built furze doors,
and ate shamrock on the run.
We played the tenora
and the penny-whistle.
We taught some policemen to read.

We've met men
who beat or even escaped
evil — even vengeance
and competition;
who saw vengeance in the mirror
and smashed the mirror—some
whose minds never even re-assembled
those broken bits of glass
dredged up from where they lay
drowned
kissing deep in despair.
People whose joy and skill
was so great, though small,
they did not need to compete.
Mourning, help, forgiveness:
have not entirely mocked us.
We've hungered, murdered, worked.
All we ask is to be left in peace
to wage our little wars.
Babies, because mortal.
Growing because dying.

Must we then be ruled
by men who talk and act
as if they'd never been
seen
known
or dreamt?

let alone listened;
or danced.
                        dublin: 5/6 december 1970

Pub Song

for Macdara Woods

There was an old fiddler who stood in the street,
    charming the birds of the sunlight and snow;
and when he got pecked by the cold birds of rain,
he thought it was time to go inside again,
        so he found him a hospital bed, and he'd go—
            in he'd go!

But first he thought best to make sure of some heat,
    so he paid a barkeep for a gold baby Power;
then propped up in his bed in the old public ward,
he opened the bottle he just could afford,
        for a nightcap, a comfort, a cure!

But what had the playful bold vintners been at
    only filled up his bottle with bright lemonade!
So the bright turned to dull, and the warm turned to cold,
there was grime on the heart, there was lead over gold,
        and the practical joke was well played—
            was ill made.

Meanwhile in the house of the parish priest,
    the publicans famished their fill:
there was lashin's of water and crusts at their feast—
ach níor bhlaiseadar Muire, 's ní fheaca siad Críost—
        but they joked with a hearty good will
            (make you ill).

Now they'd never have played such a prank on a priest
    or a man with a stake in society,
but a man who makes music's a tinker at best
in the eyes of the demon those blind fools caressed,
        and so a fair butt for their piety.

By a thousand blind tinkers may their tills all be fleeced,
    their decanters all filled up with piss;
may they get the constrictions and not be released,
ná mblaise siad ól is ná bhfeice siad Críost—
        oh Mary, their opposite, grant them the kiss!

Death-Washing

Sometimes if you hear of a death
in the morning, before washing,
it makes the very thought of such
activity seem pretentious,
implying as that does worth, hope,
chance for life and you of cleansing,
when the now unalterable fact is:
while he was alive you seldom
tried to be clean as he was clean
or help clear up his dirt a bit,
so washing now is Lady Muckdeath—
yet reconsidering you mostly
wash to go out: for a gossip
over the details of dying?
but maybe to "put forth effort
or go down in shame", for each death
becomes its own memorial, cleanses
the gone man's trying time, exacts
of some a ritual cleansing,
of others only a natural, but of all.

Belfry-Hunting

for Eiléan Ní Chuilleanáin

"Hunting belfries, like belling stags,
with beaters, from coverts, with shotguns,
with bows and arrows, with all that is bestial
but in us redeemed for this inanimate stone
we bring alive by hunting it.

Some do it with butterfly-nets,
hunting belfries with butterfly-nets,
they claim to see the noble towers
veering and weaving, or resting with upright wings,
sun-heat of centuries vibrant in
the grey-gold silent stone—more musical
than any bell—as membraned wings
are sun-suffused a single season,
the grey-gold stone like insects
living on honey —"

                         "Fritillaries,
vanessas, brimstones, Ambrogio,
Sant Climent de Taüll, a hillside
over a church in a stag-melodious glen,
cicadas:
'a tremble of light in the leaves',
the green-gold close-cluster of parasol-
pines on a headland the boat coming into
Palma harbor in the early morning —"

                                   "Prou!
Recostracullóns!   We have no room, I tell you,
for tourists and postcards, or coy
self-acclamatory poems, our sport is ancient
but never permitted the fantasies of tapestries,

we're Muslim-bigoted against the figurative,
the Anti-Stone-Sport League will never know it
but what we hunt is peace, and that requires
tenacity, sobriety, and eyes
but not for pictures.   And the lepidopterists,
although we indulge them as affiliates,
are not card-carrying members, little better
than you or those Cockney upstarts
in the West Country who glimpsing a belfry
start in a flurry across the road
would run it down for dinner, not knowing
a car-killed belfry has no proper clang.

We are the only serious ones:
with bows, arrows, guns,
we're hunting and poaching for peace.

The Jailing of Devlin

They're against her because they're men
who think men are better than women.
They're against her because they're old
and she's young.
They're against her because they fear death,
as anyone with any sense does,
and because their fear of death
does not mean a liking for life.
They're against her because they fear freedom,
which no-one with any spirit does,
they confuse freedom
with chaos,
because they can't imagine, though she can,
a freedom free of chaos.
They're against her, I've little doubt,
because of her long hair and her short skirts.
Why should young women
not wear long hair
and short skirts?
Why should young women
not wear trousers?
Why should old men
in antiquated wigs
not wear short skirts?

28 june 1970
dublin

Ageing

As in convalescence,
cake tastes like bread
and bread like dust.
But this is no convalescence,
only a deepening malady.

Travel was adventure,
is now ordeal.
Arrival is all,
and even then . . .
Journeys cannot be faced
without a companion:
so too many journeys
remain unmade.

Once I knew I'd speak
all tongues, and visit
every continent.
Mexico is dying,
Rumanian still stuck
at lesson eight.

Sex needs long warning,
and even then . . .

A little adulation
from the young supplies
the needful deceit-zest
to go on dying.
Their generosity
turns mean in my mouth.

Shame at physical
blemishes dulls: I no longer
long to wear a yashmak.

I stole a march and you stole a coaster; black to a bright room

I thought you were the water,
    I thought I was a barge:
we drank our health at every lock
    and chickpeas free of charge.

I knew you were a smoker,
    and I was cannabis:
if rozzers learn their lessons wrong,
    we can't go on like this.

I felt you were a finger,
    I felt I was a nail:
and if we keep on scratching hard
    we'll end up in the jail.

I knew you were a dancer,
    I hoped I was the dance:
if I keep on like this I'll end up
    reading "True Romance".

I thought you were a drinker,
    I thought I was a snug:
who ever heard the mantis die
    on a sheepskin rug?

I thought you were a boarding-house,
    and I was both the lodgers:
Rackrent came round, we left a note:
    "Fuck the begrudgers".

I dreamt I was a nightmare,
    I dreamt you kept me sane:
I counted planets by drops of sweat
    on the fractured counterpane.

I dreamt you were like Easter,
    and I was like the tomb:
done was the battle on the dragon grey
so I stole a march and you stole a coaster
and by bush out of bourbon we both went back
    to rise in a sundark room.
(Rise and fall,
            fall and rise,
                        rise and fall
                                    in a sundark room)

A True Story

When the liberator loved humanity (for all the dictators were dead, like west britons in Ireland or crackers in Georgia), a writer was sent to jail for sleeping with his fellow-men. That was about the time all those like him were rounded up—except the few that escaped the ice-box—and marched through the city with W on their backs meaning *warm*.

His time done, the writer came out and wrote a book, not about things like that. A lenient nation considered him purged of his warmth, so the book could be published. It even won a prize—the biggest prize a grateful nation confers.

When the day for giving the prize came round, they held a jamboree. And when the writer, so recently out of grace but now covered in glory, was called up to get his prize, the chairman who gave it to him was the judge who'd sent him to jail.

So the writer climbed onto the platform and, putting his arms around the chairman (or judge) in time-honored civic-tepid style, he kissed him not in time-honored tepid style on both cheeks but warm and full on the mouth. With a resounding smack.

Like Trees, like Islands

I kneel to fasten your shoes.
I kneel, creaking, clicking.
We seem near.
Blade, thong, buckle.
I know by which notch
takes easy entry
how swollen, how tired, how rested.
How near we seem—like trees, like islands.
Like trees on their neighboring islands
that cannot uproot themselves and walk—
no kneeling fingers—
on water to meet. But moved
by an occasional strong wind
they touch branches, tangle, may even
break each other. As long
as life, the heart tholes.
They know, in a way then, how near
their islands are. Swap nests.
Trunk-tug is too strong
for any thong not to give soon.
The meeting lasts only a minute,
but these minutes recur,
and in that minute the trees congress
their different bird-song, squirrels, iguanas,
climbing, swarming, crawling life,
fruits and flowers if any.
They can even share lightning.

I kneel to fasten your shoes.
We seem near.

Connemara

for Luis Cardoza y Aragón

Much good may it do me to steal prayers from Isaac
of Nineveh; much good to recall one drunken summer
afternoon when a greengage-tree glowed like God;
much good, an infinitesimal white fish-bone
prised from my throat and gleaming in the penumbra
of a doctor's room and whiter
than any whiteness while the traffic roared,
the pulsing unbearable decibels of July sun,
outside the ajar shutters—for what does all that prayer
come down to now but mere fear.
                    I stand, Cois Fharraige, watching
two swans and four geese on grey water
under a grey sky, lichen black or mustard
on grey and rust-colored rocks, by the road-side
a knee-high yellow pole with a red band at the top
luminous at night: there must be a prayer here
but all I can catch is fear: I pray, quite panic-stricken,
to God to keep my ageing, weakened bowels closed
until we reach a hotel, I writhe in ludicrosity, beseech
the cough not rack. Still fear, and worse than ever.
(The fear of decaying food in a widowed bachelor kitchen.)
I pray against barbed wire.

In kelp cormorant fuchsia foxglove country,
collies and black-faced cream-wooled sheep,
drystone walls at once darker and brighter after the rain,
the quartz gleaming whiter in the gloaming,
I name Ben Gorm, Blue Peak, tingling day-luminous blue
in the distance, green close-to at Leenaun, I name
Lough Doo, Black Lake, Málaga-blue in the distance, harsh
blackish near-to. There must be prayers here,
I whinge against the barbed wire
of disablement, panic.

Seborrhea, cellulitis, rumplefyke.
Amylozene, Grunovit, Kaopectate.

I throw a dandelion down into the green-brown
stream of a nameless waterfall,
I watch—the right, lovely sound for a lovely meaning—
the yellow flower swirl aside out of the current,
amid mild suds be calm.
                      I pluck and throw
a second one down, it drifts under the bridge
back towards the fall. Hirpling to the other side
I crane over, peer; the flower does not appear.
Am I praying? Offering? Perhaps I'm praying
a true prayer.

Under the conical menace of a Gothic mountain,
in these green fields I pray against barbed wire,
and never forget to take my pills.

Sometimes Feel

Like an old, wrecked sponge-diver leaking,
like a suit-of-armour leaking,
like a tree-stump leafing
after the shameful white has darkened over,
like an unwashed potato brutally cut,
the sickly off-white spattered
with dark patches of decay.

Homage to José Martí

The Spanish bishop covets
pillars for his altar:
in my church, on the hill,
elm is altar.

Floor is fern,
walls birch,
the light comes down
from the blue ceiling.

At night the bishop
goes out to sing;
he rides, in silence,
on a pine-kernel.

I sleep sound
on a stone bed;
a bee grazes my lips,
and in my body the world grows.

Tell the blind bishop,
the old bishop of Spain,
to come to my church
on the hill.

A Rose and a Book for Sant Jordi

Brave Galinsoga strode up the aisle,
pocket tyrant of a half-cowed country,
the only beautiful thing about him his name,
and called, as the people were singing to God in their own language,
what they were singing in
shit. Proud Galinsoga, the boss-man's countryman,
the overpaid hireling, the white-collar jackboot-in-office,
called the word loud and clear, over and again,
just as the people were learning, at last, again,
the almost-forgotten, almost-undreamt-of feeling of freedom to sing
to God in their own language.
He got as far as the altar-rails, and then they seized him and threw
    him out.
Next day both to his private mailbox and his editorial office
there came an avalanche of little gift-packets
neatly tied in pink or yellow ribbons
containing small turds,
it being the national day, the day of Sant Jordi,
and the custom having been and beginning to be again, a bit,
to sing to God in their own language,
on that day, their day.

Galinsoga: beautiful nine-letter name.

Ode to the Future

for Brian Lynch

How wrong, how stupid, to gibe
"living in the past":
the past is alive in us now.

When I order a Smithwick and pep,
and the rude barman, serving, says
"God that must make it taste awful!"
Croesus is boiling a lamb and a tortoise
in a bronze oracle-testing pot,
thousands of Spaniards are drinking, tricept,
thimbles of potent Pipermint,
a man called Josep, called dead—
oh truly dead, oh my darling Queralt,
far from your high native rock—
is saying to me, in his Perpinyà garden,
under the bees and the jet-planes,
over the wine and the pigeon-in-cabbage,
"he donat la meva vida al amor dels amics":
I gave my life to loving my friends.

When I gulp coddle, the bacon tender, the milk tough,
with a tough, tender, young widow,
Peter is planting his pine,
I hear Des, in his speckled gansey and green beret,
ordering whiskey-and-pep, demanding
"What'll you have, Pearse?" exhorting "That'll
settle your stummick", when we clink glasses tá
"an iolar i mbárr na píne,
's an traona sa neanntóig", Cervantes and Sancho
are riding Clavileño, the wooden Pegaso,
Symons calling Ibsen "a giant who can fly",
and Unamuno is mocking,
                              single-handed,
the mockers last of all.

Whenever I smell a rose I hear
a trandafír breathing.

When I clutch you, Abelard would envy me,
and I would envy Cavafy,
the new broad spear Shaka invented
goes down before the guns,
the claymore crumbles at Culloden,
the furze doors part,
a Chinese poet, parting, says:
dasz einer des andern Freund sei,
and I remember a friend's cool, brave, loving kiss
in a crowded bar off the Haymarket,
and the beautiful, sudden, brief coolness of his body
when he came back, one morning, to the warm bed.

The past is alive in us now,
near to its high native rock.

The black and white of this world

    Kuruntokai praises a flower:
        petals white, stem black—
    women wear it in their hair.

        We need that flower,
    and we need another:
        petals black, stem white:
    for men to wear in their hair.

    A black-petalled,
        white-stemmed flower
    for women's hair.

        A white-petalled
    black-stemmed flower
        for men to wear.

Bright after Dark

for Sebastian Ryan

In the first country,
what you must do when the cow stops giving milk
is climb, after dark, a certain hill,
and play the flute: to kill your scheming neighbor's curse.
If you can find a silver flute to play,
the spell will break all the faster, the surer.
But silver is not essential.   But: the job must
be done after dark:
otherwise, it won't work.

In the second country,
when you send a child out of the house at night,
after dark, you must, if you wish it well,
take, from the fire, a burnt-out cinder
and place it on the palm of the child's hand
to guard the child against the dangers of the dark.
The cinder, in this good function, is called aingeal,
meaning angel.

In the third country,
if you take a journey at night, above all
in the blind night of ebony, so good for witches to work in,
you dare not rely on fireflies for light,
for theirs is a brief, inconstant glow. What you must hope
is that someone before you has dropped grains of maize
on the ground to light your way; and you must drop
grains of maize for whoever comes after you:
for only maize can light the way on a dark night.

Lovers

You with full hands
keep them closed, like fists;
use the warm wealth you clutch in there
only for loading blows;
a hundred birds in a cage on the latch:
none of the birds can fly.
But at times you forget, relax,
the knuckles unwhiten,
a grain of warmth slips out between fingers.
Feathers move gently.

While I advance vainly, blowing my top,
professionally proffering my open
wide wide open palms,
for all comers to lick.
Splayed. Eager. Empty.
Not even a tearlet of sweat.
Would-be generous, poor.

It still happens

Try to forgive this: I once found you gentle—
believing that the greatest thing to be—
and told you so: a strong hand thwacked the counter:
"I want more to be violent!" Oh you were gaily drunk;
but have achieved, soberly, that gay wish.

Now my excess demand for gentleness
and your impatience drive us both to violence
only unearthly gentleness might cure;
the courtesy that, once a week, for a second,
we grant each other, may seem frail to critics.

But wears the years down well: it still happens.

Notes

page 10: The Gaelic means, in verse 2: The Gaelic is less than the water in that glass; in verse 3: I speak with strangers. I believe it's right to be speaking with strangers. (Strangers, here, has the sense of outlanders, foreigners, runners-in.) In verse 4: Ah, son: don't be breaking a boat. This last was said to my friend Liam Brady in Carraroe.

page 13: The Gaelic sentence the painter spoke, in my hearing, means: You think I am out of my mind. That the "you" is plural is plain in Gaelic, though not in what Auden calls "the Oxonian dialect". The Dublin "yous" or the Munster "ye" would be clearer.

page 15: For the "tibi" in the dedication, see Catullus, who isn't otherwise relevant. I use it to address Cornelius Kavanagh, in and about whose parents' home these lines were written when he was two.

page 23: merkin: U.S. term for a pubic wig; nobilities: in parts of Spain male genitals are called "noblezas"; a cristazos limpios: Franco's bully-boys used this term themselves; it means with clean Christ-blows, or Christings.

page 26: The Gaelic line in verse 4 means: But they didn't taste Mary and they didn't see Christ; and in verse 6: may they never taste drink and never see Christ. This Gaelic is for rhyme and macaronic.

page 27: This phrase "put forth effort or go down in shame" is from 'Henderson the Rain-King', by Saul Bellow.

page 28: "a tremble of light in the leaves" is adapted from Unamuno. Prou: Catalan for enough, basta! Recostracullons: a bilingual oath I first came across in the Valencian Blasco Ibáñez's novel 'La Barraca'. Costra is Castilian for crust, and cullons (with strong emphasis on the second syllable) is a frequent exclamation in Barcelona; the literal meaning is "balls". The composite word would have much the same effect as the French remerde/outremerde.

page 30: This was written the day after she was arrested.

page 38: Martí (Havana, 1853—Dos Ríos, 1895), who died for the freedom of Cuba, wrote a book of poems called 'Versos Sencillos', from which came the words of the song 'Guantanamera', and from the longest poem in which I've taken these verses.

page 39: Sant Jordi (Saint George) is the patron saint of Catalonia, and on his feast-day the custom is for friends and lovers to give each other a rose and a book.
page 40: The Gaelic lines in verse 3, from a poem by Seán Ó Neachtain, Roscommon poet and novelist (1655-1728), mean: The eagle's on top of the pine-tree and the corn-crake's in the nettles. In verse 4, trandafír is one of the Rumanian names for a rose.
page 42: Kuruntokai is a collection of Tamil love-poems.
page 43: The first country is Transylvania; I read a book about it twenty years ago and, to my shame, I've forgotten both title and author. The second country is Ireland, my authority Dinneen. The third country is Guatemala, which I read about in Luís Cardoza y Aragón's 'Guatemala: en las líneas de su mano' (Fondo de Cultura Económica, Mexico).